Milly, M  and BB Brown

"We may look different
but we feel the same."

BB Brown was a thief.

He helped himself to lunches, when he thought
no one was watching.

BB Brown went through desks

and pockets, when he thought everyone was
out to lunch.

He took his punishment standing up

and sitting out.

Miss Blythe did her best to reform him.
"You can change your way," she said.

But BB Brown didn't change his way.

One day Miss Blythe said, "I'm calling the police."

"I'll show you the life of a thief," said the
policeman. "Come with me."

Milly and Molly went with BB Brown.
They met Gambler

and Pistol.

They met Bullseye

and Crooksy.

But the worst thief of all was Broken Nose Bill.

"Hey, you," he said to BB Brown.
"Do you want a life like mine?"
"No," BB Brown replied softly.
"Believe me, we make our own lives," said
Broken Nose Bill.

"The prison cat is the only true friend I have,"
he said sadly.
"You can change your way."

"You can change your way," said the policeman.

"You can change your way," said Miss Blythe.

BB Brown was tempted to steal but he
remembered what Broken Nose Bill had said.

When his report card was covered with stars
he gave it to the prison cat.

"Please give this to your friend Broken Nose
Bill and tell him I've changed my way,"
he said.

BB Brown walked away with his friends
Milly and Molly.
He never forgot Broken Nose Bill but he
never ever saw him again.